SPRINGDALE PUBLIC LIBRARY
405 South Pleasant
Springdale, Arkansas 72764

REBUILDING IRAQ

By Sheila Rivera

WAR IN IRAQ

SPRINGDALE PUBLIC LIBRARY
405 South Pleasant
Springdale, Arkansas 72764

WAR ★ IN IRAQ

VISIT US AT
WWW.ABDOPUB.COM

Published by ABDO & Daughters, an imprint of ABDO Publishing Company, 4940 Viking Drive, Suite 622, Edina, Minnesota 55435. Copyright ©2004 by Abdo Consulting Group, Inc. International copyrights reserved in all countries. No part of this book may be reproduced in any form without written permission from the publisher.

Printed in the United States.

Edited by: Cory Gunderson
Contributing Editors: Christopher Shafer, Paul Joseph
Graphic Design: Arturo Leyva, David Bullen
Cover Design: Castaneda Dunham, Inc.
Photos: AP/Wide World, Corbis

Library of Congress Cataloging-in-Publication Data

Rivera, Sheila, 1970-
    Rebuilding Iraq / Sheila Rivera
      p. cm.--(War in Iraq)
Includes index.
Summary: Provides background on the events leading to the beginning of Operation Iraqi Freedom and discusses the economic, political, and physical rebuilding that has been going on since the end of the major fighting.
    ISBN 1-59197-498-4
   1. Iraq War, 2003--Juvenile literature. 2. Iraq War, 2003--Engineering and constructions--Juvenile literature. [1. Iraq War, 2003. 2. War--Economic aspects.] I. Title. II. Series.

  DS79.763.R585 2003
  956.7044'3--dc22

2003058178

Table of Contents

Before the War 4

The War 8

Returning to Peace 14

Help from around the World 17

Building a New Government 23

The Iraqi Governing Council 28

Physical Rebuilding 32

Humanitarian Aid 36

Cost of Reconstruction 40

Web Sites 43

Timeline 44

Fast Facts 46

Glossary 47

Index 48

BEFORE THE WAR

On September 11, 2001, terrorists hijacked four commercial airplanes in the United States. The hijackers crashed the airplanes, deliberately killing thousands of people. Two of the airplanes smashed into the World Trade Center buildings in New York City, New York. Another crashed into the Pentagon building near Washington, D.C. The fourth airplane went down in a field in Pennsylvania.

After the attacks, U.S. president George W. Bush declared a war on terrorism. He said that the United States would seek out terrorists and those who supported them. They would be stopped.

President Bush believed the country could not wait for another terrorist attack before taking action. He wanted to catch the people who planned the September 11 attacks. He also wanted to prevent other attacks from happening.

The U.S. government considered the actions of leaders from several countries. Based on their actions, Bush named Iran, Iraq, and North Korea as threats to peace. He said something had to

Pedestrians look on as smoke billows from the World Trade Center towers in New York City.

be done to stop these countries from buying or creating weapons of mass destruction.

President Bush first concentrated his efforts on Iraq. He claimed that this country was creating weapons of mass destruction. He also believed that Iraq supported terrorists. Bush said Iraqi president Saddam Hussein had given money to terrorists, and that he had let them operate from Iraq. In addition, Bush believed that Iraq had weapons that were banned by the United Nations (UN). Most countries are members of the UN. The organization's goal is to promote peace among nations.

The UN had passed several resolutions requiring Iraq to give up its weapons of mass destruction. It had also forbidden Iraq from having any weapons that could travel a distance of 93 miles (150 km) or farther.

During the 1990s, UN weapons inspectors searched Iraq for weapons of mass destruction. The inspectors left Iraq in 1998 because Iraqi officials would not cooperate with them.

In November 2002, the UN passed Resolution 1441. It gave Iraq 30 days to reveal any weapons of mass destruction it had. UN weapons inspectors returned to Iraq the same month.

Iraq did not want to comply with the requirements of the resolution. The Iraqi government destroyed several weapons, but President Bush was not satisfied. He thought that Iraq had more weapons of mass destruction.

WAR ★ IN IRAQ

The United States asked the UN to support military action against Iraq if Saddam did not cooperate with Resolution 1441. Some UN member countries did not think military action was necessary. France, China, and several others wanted to give Iraq more time to reveal and destroy its weapons.

Bush asked world nations to support the United States in military action against Iraq if Saddam did not comply. Forty-eight nations supported U.S.-led action against Iraq. The group became known as the Coalition of the Willing.

On March 17, 2003, President Bush sent a warning to Iraq's president, Saddam Hussein. Bush told Saddam and his sons, Uday and Qusay, to leave Iraq within 48 hours. Bush said that if they did not leave Iraq, the United States would take military action.

Saddam and his sons did not leave Iraq. Coalition forces attacked Iraq on March 19, 2003. The U.S. government called the conflict Operation Iraqi Freedom.

Before the War

THE WAR

Operation Iraqi Freedom began with an air assault on a Baghdad compound. Baghdad is Iraq's capital city. A source inside Iraq had told U.S. officials that Saddam, his sons, and other Iraqi leaders were at the compound. The source said these leaders would be meeting there for several hours.

U.S. and coalition forces pounded the compound with bombs. They hoped to remove Saddam and the other Iraqi leaders without harming civilians. The results of the bombing were unknown to U.S. officials.

The military conflict in Iraq intensified over the following weeks. Coalition forces bombed government buildings. Air strikes and missiles bombarded specific sites in Baghdad. They cleared the way for ground forces, which moved steadily toward Baghdad from Iraq's borders. Convoys of armored vehicles moved in lines toward the capital. Coalition forces took over cities on the way.

Bombs and missiles destroyed presidential palaces, government offices, and intelligence headquarters in Baghdad. Some Iraqi

Iraqi citizens pass the remains of a government building destroyed during Operation Iraqi Freedom.

troops surrendered to coalition forces. Others abandoned their military uniforms and gave up their weapons. Key Iraqi officials were killed.

On April 3, 2003, U.S. forces drove tanks into downtown Baghdad. Iraqi special forces fought U.S. troops for control of the main presidential palace.

The next day, U.S. airplanes dropped bombs over Saddam International Airport. Then ground forces took over. Once in control of the airport, the coalition renamed it Baghdad International.

On April 5, U.S. forces invaded the headquarters of Saddam's elite Republican Guard Medina division. No Iraqis fought to defend it. Guns and vehicles left by Iraqi troops lay strewn throughout the base. U.S. troops destroyed the Iraqi military vehicles.

During the seizure of Baghdad, the headquarters of Saddam's political party was demolished. That group was called the Baath party. By April 9, coalition forces met little Iraqi resistance. It was clear that Saddam had lost his following. U.S. sergeant Ray Simon said of the lack of resistance in Baghdad, "I think we have broken their back. I really think this thing is almost over."

On May 1, President Bush declared that combat in Iraq had ended. U.S. and coalition troops stayed in Iraq, but it appeared that Saddam's regime had fallen. More and more Iraqi officials surrendered to coalition troops or were killed.

Freeing the Iraqi people did not come without a price. Newly liberated people took to the streets. They celebrated and shouted their opinions without fear. Some were angry about the oppressive regime they had lived under for so long. They began taking back what they thought they deserved. Lawlessness broke out as people looted Saddam's palaces. The looting increased as banks, museums, and hospitals were ransacked.

With violence and robberies increasing, some people were afraid to go to work. They were afraid to send their children to school. People were afraid to leave their homes at night.

Both coalition forces and Iraqi civilians caused destruction in Iraq. During the bombing, coalition forces knocked out electricity and telephone systems in some areas. Water treatment plants were not working. Many people did not have clean drinking water. When violence broke out among Iraqis, civilians damaged the buildings that provided them with services. This caused great problems for the Iraqi people.

Iraqis rest on a sofa taken from the destroyed city hall building in Basra, Iraq.

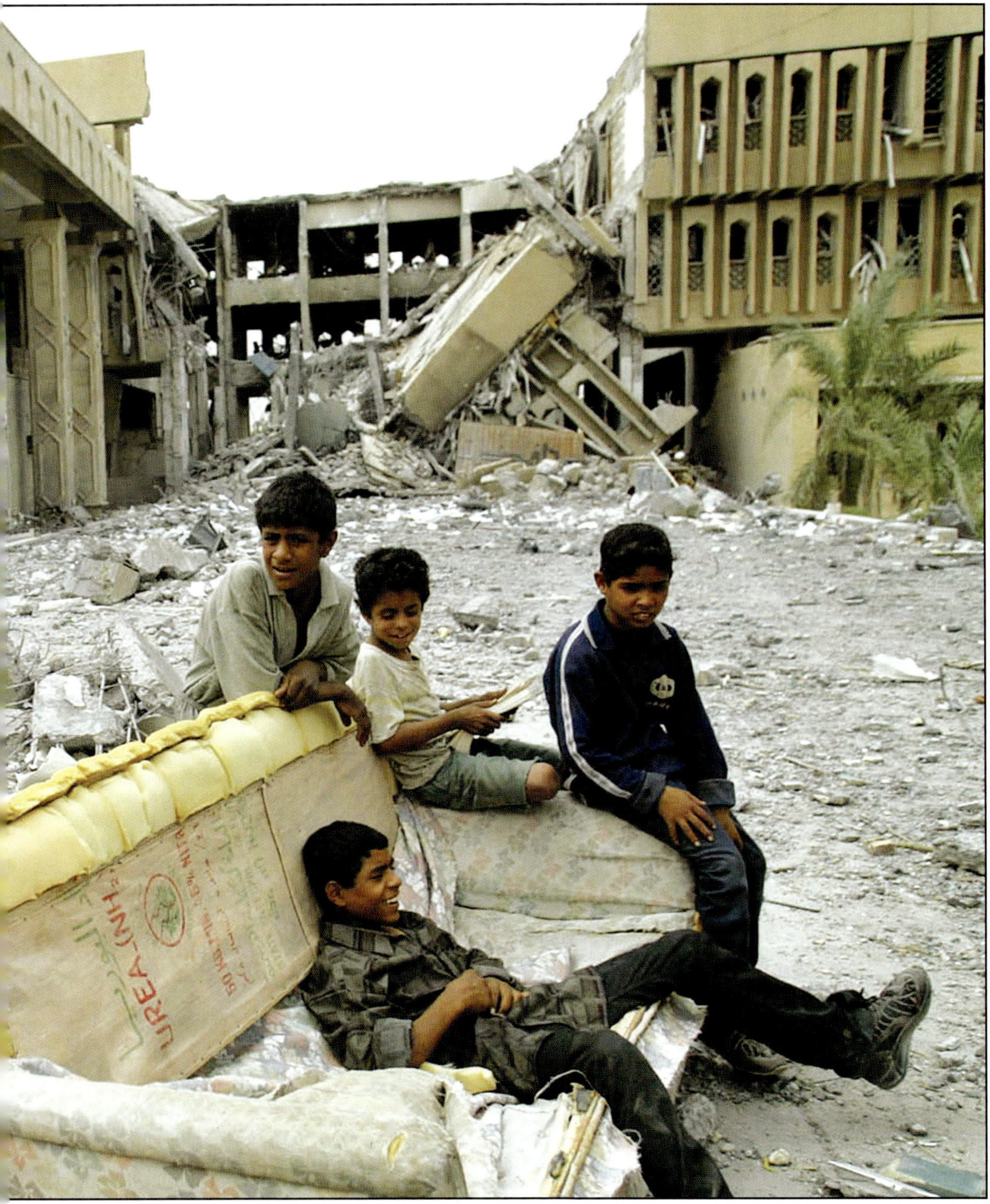

RETURNING TO PEACE

The U.S. war strategy included plans to rebuild Iraq. Coalition leaders thought about both economic and physical reconstruction. They arranged the distribution of humanitarian aid. They also planned to replace the government in Iraq.

The first priority, however, was to restore law and order in Iraq, especially in Baghdad. The fighting and stealing had to stop. People had to feel secure in their cities. They needed to go back to work, and their children needed to return to school. Without order, nothing else could be accomplished.

According to the Geneva convention, the occupying government was responsible for restoring public order and safety. In Iraq, these were the obligations of the United States.

Though President Bush had declared an end to combat on May 1, restoring order was not easy. Iraqi resistance fighters had resumed their attempts to frustrate coalition forces. Each day, coalition soldiers suffered between 12 and 20 attacks. This made some Iraqis fearful that Saddam's old regime still had power.

U.S. Marines arrest looters in Baghdad and try to restore order to the area.

WAR IN IRAQ

Then on July 22, coalition forces led a raid on a house in Mosul. Saddam's sons, Uday and Qusay, were inside the house. Both sons died in the raid. Coalition leaders hoped this would hurt the resistance movement.

Some Iraqis, however, distrusted the news that Uday and Qusay had been killed. To prove it, coalition forces released photographs and videotape of Uday and Qusay after they had died. "Now, more than ever, all Iraqis can know that the former regime is gone and will not be coming back," said President Bush after Uday and Qusay's death.

Despite the resistance attacks, coalition forces did make progress in restoring order. Iraqi police officers returned to work, and they were joined by thousands of U.S. military officers. Jails reopened. People were arrested for looting and other crimes. Having law enforcement officers in place again brought the country closer to calm.

While order was returning, coalition forces worked to restore electricity, water, and telephone services. In some areas, electricity and clean water had been lacking even before the war. Aid organizations distributed food, water, and other necessities. The rebuilding of the cities would follow.

REBUILDING IRAQ

HELP FROM AROUND THE WORLD

When the United States began the war in Iraq, it had the support of many world nations. Some nations—such as Australia, Poland, and the United Kingdom—sent soldiers to the Middle East to fight alongside U.S. soldiers. The Czech Republic sent a chemical and biological warfare support unit to Iraq. It would help coalition forces in case the Iraqi military used those types of weapons. Fortunately, that didn't happen.

Other nations offered postwar aid. Australia, Japan, Norway, and the European Union offered money to help rebuild Iraq. The United Arab Emirates offered a water purification system for Baghdad. Spain offered to send peace officers.

Until new laws and a new government were in place, Iraq needed a temporary government. The United Kingdom and United States took over the task.

On May 8, the United Kingdom and United States presented a letter to the UN Security Council. The letter announced the creation of the Coalition Provisional Authority (CPA). The CPA was to govern Iraq only until Iraqis could choose their own government. The CPA's job was to provide security for Iraqi citizens. It would also help distribute humanitarian aid, and rid Iraq of weapons of mass destruction.

The United States appointed a U.S. civilian, L. Paul Bremer, as leader of the CPA. Retired U.S. general Jay Garner was the temporary leader before Bremer's appointment. Bremer embraced the position, saying, "It is my responsibility as the administrator of the Coalition Provisional Authority . . . to bring security back to Iraq." According to the CPA, the United States had three goals. They were to provide security, eliminate weapons of mass destruction, and abolish the Baath party.

The United Kingdom and United States proposed a resolution to the UN Security Council on May 9. They asked for control of Iraq for a minimum of one year.

Spain, Angola, and Chile supported the resolution. Russia, France, and China thought the plan needed changes. They thought that it gave too much power to the United Kingdom and the United States. They believed that the UN should have more power in postwar Iraq. The resolution was revised.

On May 22, the UN Security Council passed Resolution 1483. It passed with a vote of 14-0. Syria's representative did

CPA leader L. Paul Bremer visits Iraq to assess Iraqis' needs.

The difference between the Iraq plan and the Marshall Plan was that Iraq already had the resources to improve its economy—oil and fertile land for farming. After World War II, the United States had to provide Europe with resources as well.

Part of the plan for Iraq included phasing out the Oil-for-Food program that had been in place since 1995. The program gave Iraq money for food in exchange for oil. It had been set up to ease the hardship of Iraqis due to sanctions.

Sixty percent of Iraqis were dependent on the program for food. But if Iraq's industry increased, the country could support its citizens without the Oil-for-Food program. The UN resolution passed on May 22 lifted sanctions and approved phasing out the Oil-for-Food program by September 2003.

BUILDING A NEW GOVERNMENT

Coalition officials met with Iraqis to discuss what kind of government the Iraqis wanted. They talked about how new leaders would be chosen. They met with prospective leaders. CPA leader Bremer explained, "We are continuing our active dialogue with Iraqi leaders, we are meeting with them every day." He added, "We want a government representative of all Iraqi people."

Iraq has three main groups of people: the Kurds, concentrated in northern Iraq, the Arab Shiite Muslims in the south, and the Arab Sunni Muslims in central Iraq. The population is also divided into other religious, tribal, and political groups. The United States thought that representatives from all groups should participate in the new government.

The exception was the Baath party. Baath party members had treated Iraqis poorly under Saddam's leadership. High-ranking Baath party members were banned from participating in the new government. They were prohibited from holding other kinds of

Jay Garner addresses Iraqi officials at a meeting in Baghdad.

jobs as well. In some cases, Iraqis were required to sign letters rejecting the Baath party in order to get certain jobs.

An interim authority was needed to govern Iraq until the permanent government could be elected. The interim authority would be made up of Iraqi citizens, not U.S., British, or other coalition members. It would create a constitution and new laws, redesign the education system, and create a plan for future elections.

The United States created the Office of Reconstruction and Humanitarian Assistance (ORHA) in January 2003. It was headed by retired U.S. Army lieutenant general Jay Garner. ORHA's job was to organize the new Iraqi government, rebuild the cities, and direct humanitarian efforts.

ORHA created a four-step plan to carry out its work. The first step was to place new people in government positions that had been filled by Saddam's supporters.

The second step was to turn power over to the interim authority. ORHA thought the interim authority should have about 22 members. Most of them would be native Iraqis, with few, if any, exiles. Exiles are people who are born in one country, but have been living in another country. Most exiles leave their home countries for political reasons. Part of the job of the interim authority would be to create a new Iraqi military.

Building a New Government

The third step, about nine months into the plan, was to have a Constitutional Assembly. Iraqis would design a constitution and government system.

The fourth step was to elect a permanent government. ORHA estimated that this would happen after about two years. During those two years, the interim government would be planning and rebuilding the country.

A national conference was planned for mid-July 2003. Three hundred Iraqi representatives were scheduled to meet to elect the interim authority.

The United States and United Kingdom revised this plan on June 1. Instead of allowing Iraqis to choose the interim government, the United States and United Kingdom would choose the group. The coalition partners believed that if they chose the interim authority, it would prevent infighting among Iraqi groups. They also thought that a coalition-chosen government would be more representative of all of Iraq's citizens.

While this was a step toward a new Iraq, citizens were eager for coalition forces to leave. They were upset that the new government could not be in place sooner.

By May 15, some cities already had new local governments. In Umm Qasr, British authorities chose 12 local professionals to lead its city council. They planned an election for the following week. Citizens would then vote for permanent council members. It was the first time in nearly 35 years that the residents of Umm Qasr had any choice in their government. Many had never experienced democracy.

Iraqis celebrate the end of Saddam's rule.

Building a New Government

THE IRAQI GOVERNING COUNCIL

There were many possible candidates for service in Iraq's new federal government. While Iraqis would eventually elect their own leaders, coalition partners would select suitable candidates for the interim authority.

Coalition partners and UN members believed that Iraq's government should represent all Iraqis, not just one group. Coalition leaders met with people from the country's various regions, religious groups, tribes, and ethnic groups to get their ideas about how Iraq should be governed.

Coalition leaders spoke with Shiite and Sunni Muslims. Shiites make up Iraq's largest religious group. Shiites had been oppressed, imprisoned, and exiled under Saddam's rule. Because they represent more than half of Iraq's population, Shiites were expected to have a major role in the new government. Some Shiites wanted the new government to be based on Islam and headed by a Muslim leader. However, the coalition and many Iraqis did not support this type of government.

Iraqi Governing Council

Following are the members of the Iraqi Governing Council:

The Iraqi Governing Council held a press conference after its first meeting

- Ahmed Chalabi, founder of Iraqi National Congress, Shiite • Abdel-Aziz al-Hakim, a leader of the Supreme Council for the Islamic Revolution, Shiite • Ibrahim al-Jaafari, Dawa Islamic Party, Shiite • Naseer al-Chaderchi, National Democratic Party, Sunni • Jalal Talabani, Patriotic Union of Kurdistan, Sunni Kurd • Massoud Barzani, Kurdistan Democratic Party, Sunni Kurd • Iyad Allawi, leader of the Iraqi National Accord, Shiite • Ahmed al-Barak, human rights activist, Shiite • Adnan Pachachi, former foreign minister, Sunni • Aquila al-Hashimi, a woman, foreign affairs expert, Shiite • Raja Habib al-Khuzaai, a woman, maternity hospital director, Shiite • Hamid Majid Moussa, Communist Party, Shiite • Mohammed Bahr al-Uloum, cleric from Najaf, Shiite • Ghazi Mashal Ajil al-Yawer, northern tribal chief, Sunni • Mohsen Abdel Hamid, Iraqi Islamic Party, Sunni • Samir Shakir Mahmoud, prominent Saddam opposition figure, Sunni • Mahmoud Othman, Sunni Kurd • Salaheddine Bahaaeddine, Kurdistan Islamic Union, Sunni Kurd • Younadem Kana, Assyrian Christian • Mouwafak al-Rabii, human rights activist, Shiite • Dara Noor Alzin, judge, Kurd • Sondul Chapouk, a woman, Turkmen • Wael Abdul Latif, Basra governor, Shiite • Abdel-Karim Mahoud al-Mohammedawi, member of Iraqi political party Hezbollah, Shiite • Ezzedine Salim, Dawa Islamic Party, Shiite

Sunni Muslims are the second-largest religious group in Iraq. Saddam was a Sunni Muslim, and this group controlled the government during his regime. However, not all Sunnis supported Saddam. Sunnis were also expected to serve in the new government.

Another group the coalition met with is the Kurds. The Kurds are a non-Arab ethnic group who live in northern Iraq. They were also oppressed under Saddam's regime. Thousands were injured or killed in the 1980s when Saddam attacked them with chemical weapons. Kurds were not expected to gain national power in Iraq, but they hoped to have a voice in the new government. They wanted a federal democracy that would protect their freedom.

Another ethnic group is the Turkmen. They are a nomadic Arab tribe whose members live in many countries. There are many Turkmen in Iraq. They wished to have representation in the new government, too.

Some secular groups also wanted power in Iraq's new government. One candidate considered for the new Iraqi government was Ahmed Chalabi. Chalabi fled Iraq in 1958 and lived in exile. In 1992, he founded the Iraqi National Congress, Iraq's most well-known opposition group. Chalabi supports the effort to create a democracy in Iraq.

The royalists are another group that want a new role in the government. Among the royalist candidates are the Hashemites.

WAR ★ IRAQ

They are a family that is believed to be descended from the prophet Muhammad.

After much consideration, coalition leaders assembled the temporary government. On July 13, 2003, the members of the Iraqi Governing Council were announced. There were twenty-five members on the council, including three women. The Council consisted of 13 Shiite Muslims, 5 Sunni Muslims, 5 Kurds, 1 Christian, and 1 Turkmen.

Iraqi and coalition leaders had worked to create a government that represented all Iraqis. Each council member represents one million Iraqis. Council members will establish a constitutional assembly that will write Iraq's new constitution. Elections for government positions are expected to be held in late 2004 or early 2005.

The council held its first meeting on July 13. The first order of business was to declare April 9 a national holiday. It is in remembrance of the day coalition forces overthrew Saddam's regime and liberated the Iraqi people.

The Iraqi Governing Council

PHYSICAL REBUILDING

During Operation Iraqi Freedom, news footage showed buildings with walls destroyed by bombs and missiles. Some buildings burned, and others were nothing but heaps of rubble. In addition to the damage from the war, Iraqi schools, hospitals, roads, and bridges had suffered from 12 years of UN sanctions.

The United States and coalition partners could not leave the cities and airport in ruins. They could not leave Iraqis without basic public services. The buildings, water systems, and public offices needed to be repaired and rebuilt. Oil refining equipment needed repairs so the country could produce more oil. Many countries and private companies competed for construction projects.

During Operation Iraqi Freedom, the U.S. Army Corps of Engineers (USACE) provided technical assistance for military operations and for ORHA. One of USACE's goals was to improve oil production in Iraq. It was expected to cost $5 billion and take 18 months for Iraq to get its oil output up to pre-1991 levels. Sanctions imposed during Iraq's invasion of Kuwait stopped most

Iraqi troops burned some of Iraq's oil fields in 2003.

oil exports. The machinery used to produce oil had not been repaired or replaced since before that time.

Teams of engineers worked with the departments of electricity, water and irrigation, and housing and construction. They trained Iraqi engineers and scientists.

Many people thought the postwar reconstruction jobs should be given to Iraqis and other Middle Eastern workers. Some thought the United States should make the repairs.

The United States planned to offer $1.9 billion in contracts to construction companies. Some contracts would likely be shared with subcontractors. These are smaller companies who work for large companies. Companies from the United States, Europe, and Asia sought construction contracts. The most attractive contracts were those to rebuild Iraq's oil industry.

In April, Middle Eastern companies began competing for the multimillion-dollar reconstruction projects in Iraq. Since they had supported the coalition in the war, they expected to win some of those contracts.

Groups of companies from Saudi Arabia, Egypt, Jordan, the United Arab Emirates, and the United States met to bid on building projects. They included construction of hospitals, ports, airports, and electrical and water facilities.

A private company in the United Arab Emirates set aside $50 million, which it hoped to invest in reconstruction projects. Jordan expected to win an oil pipeline project.

An April report claimed that the United States and Asian countries had already acquired most of the reconstruction projects. Another report said that the United Kingdom and the United States were getting most of the work.

By the end of April, a U.S. company, the Bechtel Group, had won the largest contract. It was worth $680 million. Bechtel was expected to play a major role in various reconstruction projects in Iraq. Another U.S. company, Stevedoring Services of America, received a $4.8 million contract to maintain the port at Umm Qasr.

On May 23, more than 1,000 people attended a London meeting organized by the Bechtel Group. Representatives from European and Asian companies, as well as some Iraqi exiles, came to compete for construction contracts. British engineering, construction, and scaffolding companies were among the 10,000 firms expected to apply for the contracts.

HUMANITARIAN AID

As soon as the war in Iraq began, humanitarian aid poured into Iraq. The United States and United Kingdom distributed food, water, hygiene kits, blankets, and water containers.

Many other countries also offered assistance. So did nongovernmental aid organizations. Aid groups worked together to help the Iraqis as quickly as possible.

The United States sent members of the Disaster Assistance Response Team (DART) into Iraq. DART's job was to find out what kind of help the people needed, and to send groups that could fulfill those needs quickly.

DART worked closely with the U.S. Agency for International Development (USAID). USAID was created after World War II, when the Marshall Plan was designed. The department works under the U.S. secretary of state to help other countries that have been affected by disasters. It also helps countries that are trying to get out of poverty, or are working on governmental changes. In Iraq, USAID organized humanitarian aid groups.

Coalition troops unload humanitarian aid packages in Basra, Iraq.

WAR ★ IN IRAQ

The Office of Foreign Disaster Assistance is part of USAID. It was in charge of gathering supplies such as water tanks, hygiene kits, health kits, and blankets for Iraqis. It also paid agencies, such as the World Food Program and the UN Children's Fund, to work together and to position supplies inside Iraq. Many other groups worked with them.

Save the Children and Mercy Corps went to Basra and Arbil to repair water and sanitation systems. Save the Children also provided health-care aid in Mosul.

A private international organization called International Medical Corps sent volunteer doctors to Iraq. They assessed medical supply and training needs in Iraqi hospitals. They delivered medical supplies and helped local doctors perform operations.

The Red Cross helped individuals by ensuring that the wounded received medical care. It made sure that people had clean drinking water. It helped people who had fled their homes during the bombing get the supplies and services they needed. It gave packages of food to people released from detention camps so they could feed their families. It also provided telephones for people who had been separated from their families, so they could contact them.

The Red Cross helped hospitals, too. Members toured hospitals to assess their needs. They delivered blankets, water, and fuel to health-care facilities in distress.

REBUILDING IRAQ

WAR IN IRAQ

In the south, Iraqi Red Crescent volunteers taught people about the dangers of mines and unexploded bombs. Between April 10 and May 13, 18 people had been hurt or killed by unexploded bombs in the city of Basra alone. Red Crescent groups from Kuwait, Syria, and Bahrain donated food, water, medical staff, fuel, and clothing to Iraq.

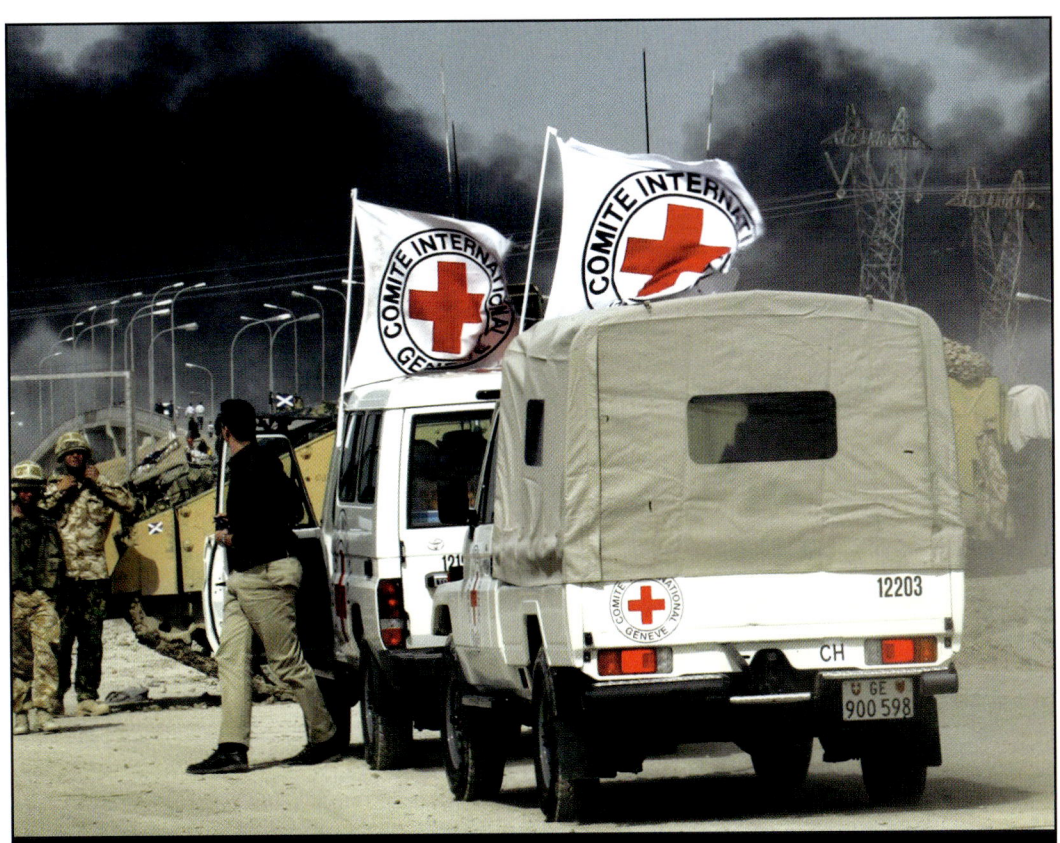

Trucks from the Red Cross approach the city of Basra to deliver medical supplies and provide basic medical services.

Humanitarian Aid

COST OF RECONSTRUCTION

The cost of war is enormous. So is the cost of rebuilding a country after a war. Sources estimated that rebuilding Iraq could range from $84–$500 billion.

Estimated costs included $6–$10 billion in payments to allies in the Middle East. Some of those countries were promised monetary rewards in exchange for their help during Operation Iraqi Freedom. Food and medical supplies could total between $1–$10 billion. Paying Iraqi police officers and workers was estimated between $5–$10 billion. Iraq's debt was between $62–$361 billion. Rebuilding the cities and industries could cost an additional $10–$105 billion.

Many of Iraq's public services were lacking even before the war. Nearly half of all Iraqis did not have safe drinking water. Seventy percent of Iraq's waste treatment plants needed repairs. Much of the country's waste was dumped into the Tigris and Euphrates rivers. These rivers are the people's water sources. Iraq's electrical system only worked at 50 percent of its capacity.

WAR IN IRAQ

Its oil production equipment was old or needed repair. It only produced a fraction of its potential. This led to gas shortages. In its poor state, Iraq could not afford to rebuild on its own. Many countries offered to help.

By April 22, the United States had already spent $25 billion on war costs. It dedicated $550 million more to reconstruction in Iraq. The United Kingdom pledged $330 million. Australia and Japan each pledged $100 million. Spain offered $56 million. The Netherlands and Norway each pledged $21 million to rebuild Iraq. Together, the donations totaled more than $1 billion.

The United States planned a donors' conference to raise additional money for Iraq. First the World Bank had to assess Iraq's financial needs.

In addition to donations, the United States had control of $1.7 billion of Iraq's money. It had frozen this money when Saddam was in power. The United States agreed to release the money so it could be used toward rebuilding.

During the war, U.S. soldiers also found $768 million hidden in a Baghdad neighborhood. Soldiers found $112 million of this money hidden in dog kennels. The remaining $656 million was found in four homes nearby. An Iraqi interpreter had been helping the U.S. troops. He said, "It makes me so sad, I see our people starving, and here these other people are hiding hundreds of millions

Cost of Reconstruction

of dollars. This is the people's money, not theirs." All of this money will be used in rebuilding efforts as well.

Coalition partners looked for ways Iraq could help with its rebuilding and recovery. Once repaired, Iraq's oil business could produce $20 billion a year in income. That money could be used to rebuild the country. It could also help raise the Iraqi people's standard of living.

Now that UN sanctions have been lifted, Iraq can begin international trading again. Once its industries increase production and the country resumes trading, the economy will surely improve.

Since Operation Iraqi Freedom, the world has offered extensive assistance and humanitarian aid to Iraqi people. With help from the UN, aid organizations, and world nations, Iraq can become a democratic nation. Someday it may be a competitor in the world market.

Web Sites
www.abdopub.com

To learn more about rebuilding Iraq, visit ABDO Publishing Company on the World Wide Web at **www.abdopub.com**. Web sites about rebuilding Iraq are featured on our Book Links page. These links are routinely monitored and updated to provide the most current information available.

A shopkeeper works to rebuild his Baghdad shop after Operation Iraqi Freedom.

TIMELINE

1939–1945
World War II

1947
Marshall Plan implemented in Europe

1988
Saddam used chemical weapons against Iraqi Kurds

1990
Iraq invaded Kuwait
UN imposed sanctions on Iraq

1990s
UN weapons inspectors searched Iraq for weapons of mass destruction

1991
Persian Gulf War

1995
UN began Oil-for-Food program in Iraq

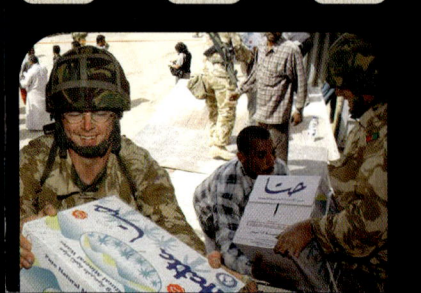

2001
September 11: Terrorists attacked the United States

2002
November 8: UN passed Resolution 1441

2003
March: Humanitarian assistance began pouring into Iraq
March 17: Bush gave Saddam and his sons 48 hours to leave Iraq
March 19–May 1: Operation Iraqi Freedom
April 9: Saddam's regime fell to coalition forces
May 8: United Kingdom and United States presented letter to the UN, announcing the Coalition Provisional Authority
May 22: UN Resolution 1483 passed
May 23: Meeting held for construction projects in Iraq
July 13: Members of the Iraqi Governing Council were announced
July 22: Qusay and Uday Hussein killed
July 24: Coalition forces released photos of Hussein brothers to prove their deaths

Fast Facts

- Iraq's population is 97 percent Muslim. About 65 percent is Shiite and 32 percent is Sunni. The remaining 3 percent of the population is Christian or another religion.

- The Kurdish people live in a region of southwest Asia called Kurdistan. Kurdistan is not an independent country. It is an area of land that includes parts of Armenia, Azerbaijan, Iran, Iraq, Turkey, and Syria.

- In 1988, Saddam used chemical weapons against Kurds in northern Iraq. It is estimated that more than 5,000 people died. Thousands more were injured or suffered long-term illness from the chemicals.

- On May 15, 2003, British officials selected 12 Iraqis to lead the city council in Umm Qasr. An earlier city council fell apart due to disagreements among council members.

- Ahmed Chalabi, the leader of the Iraqi National Congress, was considered a candidate for Iraq's new federal government. The U.S. Department of Defense supported him, but the U.S. State Department did not trust him. In 1992, Chalabi was convicted of bank fraud. He was sentenced to 22 years in prison by a Jordanian court. He returned to Iraq in March 2003.

- In late April 2003, Mohammed Muhsin al-Zubaidi declared himself the new mayor of Baghdad, Iraq. He moved into a Sheraton Hotel, and opened city offices in a country club next to the hotel. He attempted to fire employees of the electric company and hire his friends in their place. The U.S. military arrested al-Zubaidi.

Glossary

civilian: Someone who is not a member of the military.

convoy: A large group of individual units traveling together for protection.

democracy: A government led directly by the people or through elected representatives.

dictatorship: A government under which one person or group has all the power.

Geneva convention: A series of agreements that established international rules for the treatment of prisoners of war, the sick, and the wounded. The first meeting was held in Geneva, Switzerland, in 1864. The principal legal document was adopted in 1949.

humanitarian aid: Food, water, supplies, and help given by one person or group to another group in need.

hygiene kit: A package of items used for personal cleanliness, such as toothbrushes and soap.

loot: To steal in a time of crisis.

opposition group: A political party or organized group opposed to the group, party, or government in power.

Pentagon: The large, five-sided building near Washington, D.C., where the main offices of the Department of Defense are located.

regime: A government in power.

resolution: A formal decision adopted by a group.

Shiite Muslim: A member of the branch of Islam that regards Ali and his descendants as the rightful successors to the prophet Muhammad.

Sunni Muslim: A member of the branch of Islam that originally voted for the prophet Muhammad's successor.

weapons of mass destruction: Weapons that kill or injure large numbers of people, or cause massive damage to buildings. When people talk about weapons of mass destruction, they are usually referring to nuclear, biological, or chemical weapons.

Index

A
Angola 18
Arbil, Iraq 38
Asia 34
Australia 17, 41

B
Baath party 10, 18, 23, 25
Baghdad, Iraq 8, 10, 14, 17, 41
Bahrain 39
Basra, Iraq 38, 39
Bechtel Group 35
Bremer, L. Paul 18, 23
Bush, George W. 4, 6, 7, 10, 14, 16

C
Chalabi, Ahmed 30
Chile 18
China 7, 18
Coalition Provisional Authority (CPA) 17, 18, 20, 23
Czech Republic 17

D
Disaster Assistance Response Team (DART) 36

E
Egypt 34
Europe 21, 22, 34
European Union 17

F
France 7, 18

G
Garner, Jay 18, 25
Geneva convention 14

H
Hashemites 30, 31
Hussein, Qusay 7, 8, 16
Hussein, Saddam 6–8, 10, 11, 14, 16, 20, 23, 25, 28, 30, 31, 41
Hussein, Uday 7, 8, 16

I
International Medical Corps 38
Iran 4
Iraqi Governing Council 31
Iraqi National Congress 30

J
Japan 17, 41
Jordan 34, 35

K
Kurds 23, 30, 31
Kuwait 20, 32, 39

L
London, England 35

M
Marshall Plan 21, 22, 36
Mercy Corps 38
Mosul, Iraq 16, 38
Muhammad 31

N
Netherlands, The 41
New York, New York 4
North Korea 4
Norway 17, 41

O
Office of Foreign Disaster Assistance 38
Office of Reconstruction and Humanitarian Assistance (ORHA) 25, 26, 32
Oil-for-Food program 22
Operation Iraqi Freedom 7, 8, 32, 40, 42

P
Pennsylvania 4
Poland 17

R
Red Crescent 39
Red Cross 38
Republican Guard 10
royalists 30

Russia 18

S
Saddam International Airport 10
Saudi Arabia 34
Save the Children 38
Shiite Muslims 23, 28, 31
Simon, Ray 10
Spain 17, 18, 41
Stevedoring Services of America 35
Sunni Muslims 23, 28, 30, 31
Syria 18, 39

T
Turkmen 30, 31

U
Umm Qasr, Iraq 26, 27, 35
UN Children's Fund 38
UN Security Council 17, 18
United Arab Emirates 17, 34, 35
United Kingdom 17, 18, 26, 35, 36, 41
United Nations (UN) 6, 7, 17, 18, 20–22, 28, 32, 38, 42
United States 4, 7, 14, 17, 18, 20–23, 25, 26, 32, 34–36, 41
U.S. Agency for International Development (USAID) 36, 38
U.S. Army Corps of Engineers (USACE) 32

W
Washington, D.C. 4
World Bank 41
World Food Program 38
World War II 21, 22, 36